No Shelter

OTHER BOOKS BY PURA LÓPEZ-COLOMÉ

Éter es
Intemperie
Aurora
Un cristal en otro
El sueño del cazador

OTHER BOOKS BY FORREST GANDER

Torn Awake
Immanent Visitor: Selected Poems of Jaime Saenz
  (with Kent Johnson)
Science & Steepleflower
Deeds of Utmost Kindness
Lynchburg
Rush to the Lake
Mouth to Mouth: Poems by 12 Contemporary Mexican Women

No Shelter

The Selected Poems of

PURA LÓPEZ-COLOMÉ

Translated by Forrest Gander

Graywolf Press
Saint Paul, Minnesota

Copyright © 1989, 1994, 1997, 2002 by Pura López-Colomé (Spanish)
Translation Copyright ©2002 by Forrest Gander
Introduction Copyright ©2002 by Forrest Gander

Publication of this volume is made possible in part by a grant provided by the Minnesota State Arts Board through an appropriation by the Minnesota State Legislature, and by a grant from the National Endowment for the Arts. Significant support has also been provided by the Bush Foundation; the Lannan Foundation; Marshall Field's Project Imagine with support from the Target Foundation; the McKnight Foundation; and other generous contributions from foundations, corporations, and individuals. To these organizations and individuals we offer our heartfelt thanks.

A Lannan Translation Selection
Funding the translation and publication of exceptional literary works

The translations in this book are derived from the following books by Pura López-Colomé: *Intemperie,* Juan Pablos, Editor, Ediciones Sin Nombre, México, 1997; *Aurora,* Ediciones Equilibrista, México, 1994; and *Un cristal en otro,* Ediciones Toledo, México, 1989.

Some of these translations have appeared in *The Alembic* (from *Intemperie*); *Duration* ("The Cubs"); *Jubilat* (from *Aurora*); *Luna* (from *Un cristal en otro*); *TriQuarterly* ("Heartache," "I Follow You"); *Two Lines* ("Prism"); *Verse* ("The Cubs"); and *The Gamut* ("Dramatis Personae"). Several poems from this book appear in an anthology, *Reversible Monuments: Contemporary Mexican Poets*, published by Copper Canyon Press in 2001. A chapbook including some of these translations, *Aurora*, was published by Duration Press. Thanks to its editor, Jerrold Shiroma.

Published by Graywolf Press
2402 University Avenue, Suite 203
Saint Paul, Minnesota 55114

All rights reserved.

www.graywolfpress.org

Published in the United States of America
Printed in Canada

ISBN 1-55597-360-4

2 4 6 8 9 7 5 3 1
First Graywolf Printing, 2002

Library of Congress Control Number: 2001096551

Cover design: Christa Schoenbrodt, Studio Haus
Cover photograph: Nina Subin, *Hverarond, Iceland* (1997)

Contents

Pura López-Colomé

Born in Mexico City in 1952, Pura López-Colomé studied literature at Universidad Nacional Autónom de México, publishing literary criticism, poems, and translations in a regular column for the newspaper *Unomásuno*. The author of several important books, including *El sueño del cazador, Un cristal en otro, Aurora,* and *Intemperie,* she is also the translator into Spanish of works by Samuel Beckett, H. D., Seamus Heaney, Gertrude Stein, and others. Robert Hass notably incorporated lines from a poem by Pura López-Colomé in his own poem, "English: An Ode," in his book, *Sun Under Wood.* In 1998, The Academy of American Poets brought López-Colomé to New York, and the Lannan Foundation flew her to Santa Fe to give readings of her work. Most recently, Seamus Heaney invited Pura López-Colomé to Ireland, where they read together to an enthusiastic audience.

Pura López-Colomé's own poetry is philosophical and exacting, pared into short, sharp lines, obsidian flakes. Her imagination, like Paul Celan's, is marked by a kind of moral severity located in language itself; the poems are less concerned with representing the observable surface of life than with tracing melodies, the surges and diminuendos of a spiritual vision. Their difficulty and accomplishment are equally located in the collision of tones, with puns and language play juxtaposed against stark emotional revelations. "I have no interest in sincerity," she once told me. "Sincerity and veracity are distinct." Her concerns have necessitated the unconventional approach to language that marks her work, its meditative intensity, and its often dialogic form.

A Note on the Translation

I approach the self-obliterating ecstasy of translation with trepidation. The more so because my own language derives from a Europe whose history of military and economic conquests deprived so many other cultures of their indigenous languages. Translation, like all activities, takes place as part of a politics concerned with the flow of power. I may hope that my own translations are less colonial raids into other languages than subversions of English, injections of new poetic forms, ideas, images, and rhythms into the muscular arm of the language of power, but I know they are both. I look to translations to refresh American English. And translations of poems may serve also to help inoculate readers against a language of manifest destiny, the language of the *New York Times*. For one form of totalitarianism, surely, is the corralling of human feeling into uniform language.

Nicholas Kilmer, in his translations of Petrarch's *Songs and Sonnets,* points out a wonderful sentence that Petrarch, himself a translator, wrote. Petrarch believed that what the translator writes should be "similar, but not the very same; and the similarity, moreover, should be not like that of a painting or statue to the person represented, but rather like that of a son to a father, where there is a shadowy something—akin to what painters call one's air—hovering about the face, and especially in the eyes, out of which there grows a likeness that immediately, upon our beholding the child, calls the father up before us."

As a translator, I try to make something equivalent, not equal. I am not above inventing rhyme or wordplay in translation where there is none in the original in order to make up for wordplay or rhyme that is lost elsewhere. But a translator can justify such "recoveries" only as acts of faith, by translating not individual words, but the poem as a whole. Servius comments on the "fidus . . . Achates" of *Aenid* I. 188, drawing a distinction between *fidus* and *fidelis*. A translation can be merely dependable, replacing one word with another, or it can be faithful, where faith is a form of knowledge and belief.

In Pura López-Colomé's art, wordplay is an integral part of the intended meanings of the poems. When she writes, in "Los Cachorros" ("The Cubs"):

Siluetas que se arrastran
por el mármol,
el mar del mal,
la mía entre ellas.

—the words might be translated to stress semantic meaning as:

Silhouettes that drag themselves
through the marble,
the sea of evil,
my own among others.

But what would be lost in that translation is essential to the poem in Spanish. In English, we lose the rich sounds in Spanish, the repeating r's, m's, and l's. Even worse, the deformation of *mármol* into its constituent near-phonemes, *mar* and *mal*, introduces a Kabbalistic inquiry, one which is central to Pura López-Colomé's poetic project, one which links the sounds and spellings of words to orbits of mystical, moral, and spiritually—and—imaginatively transformative possibilities.

In my translation, I choose to alter the literal meaning in order to stress an equivalent degree of linguistic complication. I translate the lines as

Silhouettes dragged
through granite hills,
grey nets of hell,
mine among them.

Finally, what I would like to happen in the act of translation is an intuitive empathy by which I might feel my way into hearing the music of the mind that inhabits the original poem. I aim to recreate, sometimes in different places, the same degree of reader participation in the translation as in the original. There is no serviceable theory for this approach. As Eliot Weinberger says, "Translation theory, however beautiful, is useless for translating. There are the laws of thermodynamics, and there is cooking."

A Personal Note

I met her where? By the time we were sitting in an art gallery court-
yard in Mexico City in 1998, Pura with her head shaven, looking—if
it were possible—more intense than usual, some cross between a
Zen priest and a horned owl, and her friend, the elegant Tedi López-
Mills, gesturing with a cigarette scissored between long fingers,
both of them laughing at me for some malapropism I had just com-
mitted, we already knew each other. We were about to read in a pro-
gram organized by the Mexican Cultural Institute and Bill Wads-
worth, director of The Academy of American Poets. Six U.S. poets
and six Mexican poets crossing borders to give a series of readings.
It was there, in that courtyard, after I asked her something about
her poetics, that she told me bluntly she was not interested in sin-
cerity. That sincerity and veracity were distinct.

If, like Laura Riding, Pura López-Colomé is committed to veracity,
unlike Riding, she has continued to seek out its revelation in poetry.
Only after several years of acquaintance did I come to learn some-
thing about Pura's earlier life, the edge on which she had lived
through her twenties, the dangerous choices she swerved between,
the exigencies and their toll on her. Her past has plucked out every
trace of naïveté from her eyes. Although she has a wicked sense of
humor, she is most at ease when she is serious. I think she climbed
out of what might have been an overwhelming darkness into what
could be taken for ordinary domesticity—a husband, children, a
house, friends—on the rungs of poems, one at a time. Her husband, a
scientist, plays drums in a rock band called Las Plumas Atómicas—a
pun summoning both the atomic plume and the pen. Together they
are raising two astonishingly beautiful boys.

Monolinguism is a disease, Carlos Fuentes once said. But, he con-
tinued, it has a cure. How many languages does Pura speak? I re-
member waiting in a car in Santa Fe, after the others had stepped
out, to hear her finish reciting a long poem, in English, by Thomas
Hardy. I can also remember standing in a hall at Berkeley, where
we had gone to read together, to hear her quote a full poem by

Goethe in German. She has translated into Spanish Robert Hass, Seamus Heaney, and Virginia Woolf, among others. I was curious, when I began to work with her poems, how much she would want to be involved in the process, and I have been continually surprised at her reticence to offer critiques. It is, as far as I have discerned, her only reticence. She doesn't often "correct" my translations. Consequently, a mistake has endured, on occasion, for months in a translation to which she had given tacit approval. Because of this, I have become a more careful and a more patient translator, and I cannot but think that she intends this.

Our friendship has deepened, over five years, in letters and lately, in e-mail. In 2001, she moved with her family to England where, away from the daily sounds of her language, her language rushed out from within her, and she finished a new book. Now she is back home in Cuernavaca, just beyond that giant spider which is Mexico City. She is sitting at her desk and the children are asleep. There are marvelous trees in her mind, an inaudible music. The words on the page before her are immediate, sensual, exacting. A single vowel elicited at the turn of a line gives rise to a sequence of brilliant moments. Her intelligence glances out.

I.
No Shelter

PRISM

Those coveting health—
I saw them making their way along the worn path,
the one trailing away from the city,
a part of the world,
a part of my own wounded humanity,
a sweet apparition for whomever awaits
me, living within but apart from me,
in my thirst, in my shifting
moments of trouble and peace.
I was them. I was *myself*.

They ascend toward Chalma, the pilgrims. Knowing that, on the
way, their dry branch will break into blossom. Most are young. They
carry water, a sleeping pallet, their daily lives. A few elders. Children
on their shoulders. The sanctuary in search of its premises.

At once, with a single question,
their distant past woke up in them.
For what do they petition
the Lord they worship,
a Lord whose body
is mortified by today's exhaustion
and yesterday's misery?
To be able to go on crying in fury or impotence,
to be able to sicken or to go beyond sickness,
to be able to testify to, to endure the terrifying absence of . . .
at the very core of the horn of plenty,
to be able to forget, yes,
the seven- or eight-year-old ghost
impetuously flying without tail or string
by which it might be tugged back to earth,
to forget the future history,
the missing relinquishments to love.

That?
Oh, body, Lord and Master,
show me a tree made in your image,
synagogues, shrines, mosques,
filled out with your being.

They've made camp. Night. Groups of men over here, mixed groups
over there, women with babies and children farther off. Around the
campfires, standing, squatting. They share neither food nor coffee,
each bringing out their own dinner, without making excuse for . . .
and celebrating by sitting on the hard ground, letting the rocks
bruise their thighs, nursing the baby in front of strangers. The
warmth whelms from the nearness of arms, backs, necks, breasts;
not from fire. From blood. There are those falling asleep, those
about to, and those keeping vigil. None needs a roof.

All our fates
are measured out as breath
in the songs of stars.
A communion of luminous bodies,
I prayed in terror or envy,
a particular sequence,
a particular translation,
the joy of the indispensable.
Nothing more.

The next morning, full of admiration and rapture, I returned to
those places, hoping to breathe in the last smells of what had been
dreamt and shared. Going back as though to touch the votive stone,
the feet or hands of the worn image of some miraculous saint:

I found nothing but garbage.
The Lord's mouth agape,
his stinking breath.

II.
Aurora

To Good Shelter

    1.

The other world.

Light opened its doors to me
when what I wanted was to follow
the course of my grave
dream, ensombered,
against the flow of day.
A golden waterfall,
fine needles,
penetrated my blindness:
crystal dust,
the unseen word,
dawn.
Fresh the balance.
Fresh the brilliance.
Gift of group weddings,
paradise in the apple of science,
the true juice,
ripe pleasure.

2.

This world.

A sound sometimes dry,
metallic, at
times rubbery,
has finally taken over the morning.
Has darkened little by little
the songs of various birds,
the croak of the daily,
wind in the hedges,
the green yearning.
A man places with inexhaustible precision
one tile after another on the roof of the house.
He must be the owner.
His work is like no other,
constant, wishful, irrepressible.
That sound doesn't seem to echo
but veers off,
off toward the dawn.
Those who live below
become recurrent
voices, feeding on themselves
beneath the roof.

3.

The owner has deigned to smile at me.
The gold of his teeth
cuts my talk to the quick.
To a good day,
I would say, if I could.
To good shelter.

Aurora

I.

You construct the days,
the edifices of your life.
Speaking to things,
mixed up in them, you go,
bit by bit, through
the rhythmic waves
of dream.

I see you watching the gestures.
The acts, the nature
of miracle. Like
this, the base of your petals
begins to close.
Palpable, the pressure of absence,
under my eyelids.

II.

The wind circles
the spaces you inhabit
whispering caresses.
My hand melts
there,
where nothing
is missing.
Your skin has been cauterized
sweetly.
And you're still *alive*.

III.

Many your heavens,
plentiful your spheres
turning as one singular
open earth,
in whose center boils
the water of light.
Its remembrance brings vision
to those who, seconds before death,
want nothing.
The ear, and within,
the void's tiny echo.

IV.

Tuning up, breaking through,
quick fingers of light
passing
over the crystal keyboard.
Slow sketch,
newborn blue:
points of light gleaming
against the dark shells.

V.

Thanks to the spoke of the beginning,
I could put together, almost blurred,
the silhouettes
of perfect trees,
drunken and slender bodies;
grace stood me up
like a willow,
which is how I saw myself in the water
where thought trembled,
its poor essence shuddering
before the higher thresholds to come.

VI.

Dawn,
your eyes are the air.
They take themselves
in and become aware
of themselves in the hollow of an echo.
That, there.

You approach the world
drinking it in, for the most part,
with each breath.
You've dredged that lagoon
of smiles, surprises,
fear, weeping, mystery: and now,
from between your lips the *name* of things
is pouring.

VII.

So disposed,
the drops suspended
at the tip of each leaf
announce the heavens,
shrouds of autumn or winter
still give off an ache
to be tucked into new life:

waterfall of laughter,
the air of torrential rain in one's hair,
ceaseless tears of underground caves.

VIII.

White.
Almost snow,
and so humid
that you foresee nothing,
from your fresh corpse
you rose alone,
resplendently,
unembraceably resuscitated.

The forest, the stream, this garden
have left behind the sepulchre,
its valleys,
the swampy grassland
leading to the soul's drought.
A tear-burst
sprouts from the water-soaked branches.
Like intent serpents,
the tendrils stretch away.
Language slithers off.

IX.

Above your calm,
a drowsy veil undulates,
airily:

like a full-sailed ship
run aground in the inner bay,
my body;
yours,
the tide, always benign,
soaks us over time
to the core.
My joy is such,
that I barely begin to fathom it.

To what do you listen,
I ask,
if it isn't a song
leaving your lips,
it must be hunger, the sincere thirst
of this wailing
wall which
is the flesh.
One note from you
would have opened my ears
and eyes:
so to say,
filling me
from then on.

X.

Again an emptiness pierces everything
and converts it to an emblem,
ether, human mutability.
Nothing alters the apparent
mitigation of faith.
Happiness
is fleeting.
Dust so fine.

Just as I'm about to come across
your voice in this place lush
with natural beauty,
you, being immune,
go on, inapprehensible,
a horse stepping over
the shadow of some hoofprints
hidden in the turmoil
of my skull.

Upon transfiguring

After that haze,
the air's pure spring
opens into a ventricular flower,
fully illuminating
the passage.

Welcome.

You will pour out
a ceaseless longing,
an eternal hope,

may it happen,
may it be born,
may it be reborn.

Maybe you will figure out the expected route.
Maybe you will take the way of ardor,
free already
from your aching body.
Maybe you will open into pleasure.

You will be blessed.

Let me dream
your substance indissoluble,
touch the face of beginning,
return as myself, *to myself,*
always wakeful.

III.
No Shelter

The Cubs

1.

Storm clouds, thrown runes,
this solid summer,
patient father, fountainhead
of what comes on, continuing
what has been,
skeleton of the magnificent
commonplace.
This place.
Silhouettes dragged
through granite hills,
grey nets of hell,
mine among them.
Weeds, stubborn little flowers.
Calcium of death,
fugitive bones,
radiances.

Several tiger cubs entangled, pawing, biting each other, licking
their cuts and attacking again, playing, at the border of the un-
known with their unknowing. The tigress, in that shorn landscape,
under a shrub. Her majesty. And then suddenly, things were gone
bloody, were stricken. The mother's fur stood on end. Some fly,
some bee, some meddling insect. The body was one thing and its
concern something else. Quiet, perception, absolute freedom, the
promised way, inevitably coming undone.

2.

Purple flower with thin petals,
four pistils at the center,
motherly yellow circle.
Nucleus of annals,

nucleus of hope,
the right weight.

Four creatures, snatching a skirt of flaring yellow. Four destinies,
with their own maps, their respective charms and faults. For an in-
stant, their eyes turn to the blue sky, to the girdling whiteness, the
glory, and then they fall into the dark red river, the river nearly
black. "He had lost so much blood by the time of the autopsy that
his heart was dry." Like an apricot, the kind you eat in winter cele-
brating The Good News. *Gloria in excelsis Deo.*

3.

Voices full and masculine
raise up melodies to absence.
Echoes from the cupola and walls
are the only sound,
an unrepeatable liturgy,
a sprinkling onto the forehead
of the newborn.

Hymns of the viscera sealed
inside the world's bubble.
All is womb.
All, baptismal font.
Before them, she comes
back, back already
to her place of origin
sine qua non.
"Young men, would you
lend me a hand?"
It is necessary that the palms touch
the Covenant's edges.
Pine box,
perfect for the quick unfolding
of what *must necessarily unfold*
today,

because the weather is reflected
in the immense pools of event.

And what is your life, sorrowful one? "He who eats my flesh and
drinks my blood will live in me and I in him." Hard to swallow. One
raw, the other undistilled. I managed to control my nausea, seeing
a man who had never wept. From the bottom of earth's well, the
eyes of young tiger cubs effervesce upward. Teething, the cubs de-
vour the thigh of some fresh kill. "He who eats my flesh and drinks
my blood will never die."

4.

The blue cadavers in the snow at Chechnya.
The citrine cadavers in the Lacandonian Forest.
Tender caesarian cadavers.
Osip, Joseph, José's scintillating gaze
nailed to the back of everyone's neck,
though all he wanted was something to eat,
a piece of paper with something scribbled on it.
Library ashes and black
smoke from all the books,
all the biographies on earth,
they are lighthouses for the lifeless
bodies. Hovering over
every battlefield.

DEATH OF THE KISS

*You, prayer,
you, blasphemy,
you, razor in the prayer
of my silence.*

> —PAUL CELAN

Fons

I wanted to find you inside me,
knowing the concavities of that dark place
would give me vertigo.
I wanted, I searched out your face.
I wanted, any way I could, to contemplate
the part of you within me
that would bring along the rest
and join my mouth to yours, others,
to see how the dream goes.
To know that in all, there are two
salivas, rivers of life,
influent, influential,
to know
that I know, what I know,
fiery tongues submerged
in this sea of enigmas,
gold, bathed in gold.
The Word comes forth spoken
and it is death written down,
a divine substance eternally
kissing the sheen of a marine light.
Mors osculi
formed of loving, desiring, deciphering the pure,
the impure figure, a language that says
In the beginning
conjugated and sublimated:
I am that I am,
come to me,

approach with your mouth open,
feel my breath,
fill yourself on the Name,
open your eyes and you will see
Nothing.

Origo

I'm waiting outside the third-grade class. The exam will be oral, in-dividual: triumphant. All the world trembles. It's a test on *national language*. I've got cotton-mouth, I'm pasty, my tongue's dry. I'm all sterile gusto, stuffed and suffocating. I enter. Close the door. I go slowly up the dais. "Conjugate whatever you want in any tense." Without a second's hesitation: *to lie,* the present imperfect of my con jury. Transparent, revealed, my tongue *exulted.*

Fons

Reanimated, spirit restored,
reincorporated, body restored,
I contemplate between dreams
the scene I've stolen
like the one who took fire,
like the one who opened the devil box
out of curiosity,
like the one who saw her equal
and her life's love
were the same and so effortlessly
brought them together.
I took exactly
what was not mine,
with my eyes.
I saw the sea inside you:
on your surface, mud.
I kissed you like a shipwreck,
like one who insufflates the word.
With my lips I traveled
that entire continent,
Adam, from dirt, Nothing.
I knew myself in your substance,
grounded there,
emitting aromatic fumes,
an amatory banquet of ashes.

Origo

Agency of Inhumations. Insistently, I ask each of several people: what does it mean? Someone answers: to inter. Others advise me to keep quiet. The term obsequies. *Voice* of funeral rites. I kept thinking of humidity and later of humus, and my laughter broke loose. It appeared, the day before, in a book of natural sciences: completely decomposed vegetal matter, part of the organic soil. Slime. Inhume, to bury, so soon? Better if I could put my cheek close. Smell its smell. Although then I would exhume a yearning for corruption.

Fons

Eat the bread,
drink the wine,
and live, right?
Right.
Of word and deed.
Of deed in word.
I give my word
and it returns to my mouth.
I swallow it, digest it, retch.
How many times have I said
my spirit is nearing affliction's
peak and I don't know how
to christen the suffering
and how many others have I vomited
I'm so sorry
my most sincere condolences.
I remember, in passing,
the living water, that dazzlement,
one of many nights,
my heart beating over my chest
so its angelic rise and fall
could be seen,
the heart, pure spirit,
molded from eaten words.
It speaks of the invisible,
the ineffable forces rising and falling
from the wellspring to the terror.
A beating of wings more intense
than the stroke of a chisel.
It leaps into the throat like an echo
of power, subtle,
             un soplo en el corazón
creationary,
             a heart murmur
inviting the dream

> *los ventrículos del corazón*
and cashing life's chips in
> *the chambers of the heart.*

Enough. The pump sings:
spurting between diastole and systole.
Out, out from here.
The tongue of pleasure,
of circumlocution waits,
not the tongue of the seminal kiss
in the maw of the prophet:
"And it will come to pass in the final days,"
God says,
"that my spirit will spill across all flesh
and your sons will prophesize, and your daughters,
and your young will see visions
and your elders dream dreams."
In every one, a shard of crystal meaning.
Tower fallen over fallen man,
over the grains of sand
that assemble anew
the wailing wall,
and the parapet like *razor in the prayer* . . .
A word of Yours would suffice to heal my spirit.
Which one? The breath or the murmur?
The spirit-giving breath
or the soft sound holding forth
like wind in the leaves?
Pulsations, throbbing around the doors of the body,
open me,
around the portals of the world,
close me,
around every threshold.

Origo

One is the writing inside being, which explains why I go around consuming, conserving, transforming. That is it. The other would seek and find answers far off. It is there. But, in which should the confession be articulated? How to vent pleasure if there is no *banquet*? I've already been told this means avidly abandoning oneself to a gross indulgence. A pleasure in un-burying. Behind the screen, the vicar's mouth emits a rarefied air, something untranslatable: *Presérvame, Oh Señor, en Tu misericordia. Pues saber Tu Verdad es la Vida.* Tongues inside and outside, serpents one upon the other, touching, kissing, decaying. Their papillae are pupils in search of a face. In them, that keenest note, an ecstasy so intense it "sometimes results, accidentally, in the death of the body, a way of dying known as death by the kiss. . . ."

Fons

Naked scripture,
projector of opaline bodies.
Nights reading,
cultivation, cult of The Letter.
I pray in tongues, I murmured,
to decipher my destiny,
that dark assignment
of brilliant skin and dregs of flesh.
Fruit going rotten when it is touched,
when the finger isn't lifted from the line,
when the finger isn't lifted from the sore.
I stretch out my arm speaking
of branches, bifurcation,
inscriptions on another's
tombstone.
Arm, severed limb, amputated
from the kiss.
Salvation's tablet,
rope at the neck,
sheets tossed from the window,
an escape interwoven with veins
stretched to the point of rupture.
One after another,
my life's voices have been tied off
like clipped wings:
to mean—to stretch—to reach.
The long, the smooth parts, yes,
they defeat the distances.
But now their syllables curse me:

"Already you've understood,
you've stretched toward yourself,
even just a little;
welcome to the paradise

of perfect omissions,
to shadings dissolved in . . ."

Whom do you kiss,
whom do you touch,
to whom are you joined,
gift of fire,
ethereal slipknot?
Behind veils of silence
from the deep chamber's bed
one can hear the Beloved's word:
breath . . . soplo . . .

Origo

Calm winds filled out the sails of the boat that carried my mother, after not too long a trip, to these lands adamic with misery. There, with that imperceptible shuffle, she began learning to speak the truly essential: good morning, good evening, until later . . . She brought, her only luggage, the one small "chest" containing her dearest possession: a beautiful doll, the exact replica of the child she once had been, with some little dresses for life's special occasions: everyday clothes, Sunday clothes . . . Bearing her passage of time in her arms. I don't know whether she kissed the ground that received her, whether her mother tongue was swollen with excrescencies. God only knows how she would be integrated into her surroundings in that "New World." Not long ago, someone who often kissed her in life conducted business in what on paper they call "dry remains." So, there you have it! I always had the secret knowledge that exhume and inhume would end up meaning the same thing. Something that in a puff of laughter, human as humus, *de*hisces, *dis*perses, *dis*locates, arranges here and now my own unhinging, *dis*charges, drawn from the old dyscharge, "to shoot a weapon," an ambivalence confirmed in records from the Golden Century: *dys*charge or discharge: "shooting off" or better, "matter issuing from a wound."

DRAMATIS PERSONAE

My voice went on, its tones varying.
It paused. It believed it could not go on
and it continued.
In this manner it articulated a path
never before described,
a place of which it was part
without knowing it.
To which it returned afterward.
It opened its doors,
allowing a beginning for the ears.
The cochlea surging forward,
satiating all expectations,
penetrating the body
in whelming red.

Later your blizzard voice
from the bowers
of hibernal forests,
orchards in the tundra,
from the oak, the cedar,
and from the tamarind,
blew across the awakened ones
who continue on their way
savoring
the dry melodies
of thunder.

Heartache

Why do you wander alone
Among the ships through the camp
In the middle of the night immortal?

—ILIAD X, 139

The lake of the dead has no shore.
Vast Stygian, it is also called a river.
It flows, wary, warily,
infatuating sages and believers.
Layers of illusion, of rumor,
settle easily in the ruck:
fluent mirror
of human labyrinths.

I can feel your beginnings in this boat, I murmured.
Your planks have left marks on my hands.
Night's oars spin
the very chrysalis of horizon.

Is this the eye of water
where the goddess dunked the boy
to make him invulnerable,
brutal, indifferent?
Is this the dry,
lachrymal Word
hurling escutcheons overboard?

IV.
One Crystal in Another

. . .

A kind of inaudible music
opens the way and strips us
from within
of whatever we've come
wearing. Am I blind
or do I for the first time
behold these marvelous trees?
The fruit intensifies the colors around it,
resplendent.

Habitante Seen from Outside

The stone isn't any longer a stone.
Its word skips back to me,
unsettled, like a side-glance,
my mouth full of praise.
Motherword.

The stone weighs less than conception's
pearl, we convince ourselves
at night; the stillness
is incomprehensible.
It slips through our fingers
without wriggling and transforms;
the dark, timeless velvet,
unburdens us, helps us dispense
with explanations.
Why, then, the crying?

Whose river stones
catch your eyes, *habitante*?
Morning holds a mirror.
Here it is.

You have sown pleasure, seasons,
a red tree, a yellow one,
and some boughs are still green.
Where it comes into contact with the body,
a different sun subsists.
Burning out, its fragrance
pierces the senses, a pin
in the wind: a pearl slips off
and turns to stone once more,
without sobs,
habitante.

I Follow You

To see oneself without the world,
not to recognize oneself in the mirror.
How fragile
we are, and frail,
made only of meat and bone.
The finest feelings come clear
in the tangible memory of someone
whose appearance is already intangible.
As children,
we swallow the void,
what is yours without you,
me.
Wanting a voice to fill us,
we strain to hear echoes within
which never stop
dreaming of their origins.
Happy is she who can face
all that withdraws
and remains.

I.
Intemperie

Ansias de bienestar,
las vi recorrer el camino de costumbre,
el que va de la ciudad a alguna parte,
parte del mundo,
parte de mi adolorida humanidad,
grata aparación para quien me aguarda,
quien vive dentro de mí sin ser yo misma,
en mi sed, mis oscilantes momentos
de tribulación y paz.
Fui ellas. *Me* fui.

Suben a Chalma los peregrinos. Los que saben que la rama seca que
van cargando echará flores a lo largo del trayecto. Son jóvenes en su
mayoría. Llevan agua, un petate en que dormir y la cotidianidad de
sus vidas a la vista. Hay viejos también. Niños sobre los hombros. El
santuario avanza en busca de su sitio.

De golpe, con una pregunta
despertó su antigüedad.
¿Qué le piden al Señor
a quien veneran,
es decir,
a su cuerpo mortificado
por la fatiga de hoy
y la miseria de ayer?
Poder seguir llorando de rabia o de impotencia,
poder enfermarse más o excederse,
poder presenciar, vivir la aterradora falta de . . .
al centro del cuerno de la abundancia,
poder olvidar, sí,
al fantasma de los siete, ocho años
que arrebatado vuela sin cola o cuerda
que lo regrese a tierra,
olvidar la futura historia,
las nulas entregas amorosas.

¿Eso?
Oh, cuerpo, amo y Señor,
muéstrame un árbol creado a imagen tuya,
sinagogas, basílicas, mezquitas
cubiertas todas de ti siendo.

Se ha establecido el campamento. Es de noche. Grupos de hombres
por aquí, mixtos por allá, de mujeres con bebés y niños más lejos.
En torno a las fogatas, de pie, en cuclillas. Comparten no el ali-
mento ni el café, cada quien trae su itacate, sino la razón de . . . y la
celebran sentándose en el suelo vil, dejando que las piedras se les
entierren en los muslos, dando de mamar al niño delante de quien
sea. El calor proviene de la cercanía de brazos, espaldas, cuellos,
senos; no del fuego: de la sangre. Hay quien cae dormido, quien
cabecea, quien vela. Ninguna necesidad de techo.

Todos estamos destinados
al compás respiratorio
con que cantan las estrellas.
Comunión de astros es ésa,
recé con terror o envidia,
una cierta rotación,
una cierta traslación,
el gozo de lo indispensable.
Nada más.

Al día siguiente, llena de admiración y arrobo, regresé a esos lu-
gares, deseando aspirar los últimos olores de lo que ahí se había
soñado y compartido. Como quien vuelve a tocar la piedra votiva,
los pies o las manos de la imagen gastada de algún santo milagroso:

No hallé sino basura.
La gran boca del Señor,
su mal aliento.

II.
Aurora

A *buen resguardo*

1.

El otro mundo.

La luz me abrió sus puertas
cuando quería seguir el cauce
de este sueño
grave, ensombrecido,
en dirección contraria al día.
Una dorada catarata,
agujas finas,
penetraba mi ceguera:
polvo de cristal,
palabra nunca vista,
aurora.
Nuevo el peso.
Nuevo el brillo.
Regalo de bodas colectivas,
paraíso en la manzana de la ciencia,
jugo verdadero,
gozo a tiempo.

2.

Este mundo.

Un sonido a ratos seco,
metálico,
de goma a ratos,
ha poblado la mañana desde entonces.
Ha opacado poco a poco
cantos de pájaros diversos,
graznidos llenos de costumbre,
viento entre los setos,
esperanza vegetal.
Un hombre coloca con minucia inagotable
una teja y otra en el techo de hogar.
Debe ser el dueño.
Su tarea es como ninguna,
puntual, deseosa, irrefrenable.
Aquel sonido no parece tener eco,
va en su busca,
en busca de la aurora.
Quienes vivan debajo
serán voces que regresan,
de sí mismas se alimentan
bajo techo.

3.

El dueño se ha dignado sonreírme.
El oro de sus dientes
me ha cortado el habla de raíz.
A buena hora,
diría, si pudiera.
A buen resguardo.

AURORA

I.

Construyes los días,
los edificios de tu vida.
Hablando con las cosas,
te vas metiendo en ellas
paso a paso,
entre las olas cadenciosas
del sueño.

Te veo ver el movimiento.
Los actos, la naturaleza
de milagro.
Se va cerrando así la base
de tus pétalos.
Palpo entre mis párpados
su ausencia.

II.

El viento ronda
los espacios que tú habitas,
susurrando caricias diferentes.
Mi mano se derrite
ahí,
donde no hace falta
nada.
La piel se te ha cauterizado
dulcemente.
Y sigues *viva*.

III.

Muchos son tus cielos,
tantas tus esferas
girando en una sola
tierra abierta,
en cuyo centro hierve
el agua de la luz.
Su recuerdo da la vista
a quien no deseaba nada
segundos antes de la muerte.
El oído, y dentro,
el eco breve de una gruta.

IV.

Se entona, rompe,
despunta el paso
de ligeros dedos
sobre el teclado de cristal.
Dibujo lento,
azul recién nacido:
sus puntos ya se encienden
tras las cáscaras oscuras.

V.

Gracias al rayo del principio
pude hilvanar, casi esfumadas,
las siluetas
de los árboles perfectos,
cuerpos ebrios y sutiles;
su gracia me fue alzando
como un sauce,
como tal me vi en el agua
donde temblaba el pensamiento,
su pobre ser estremecido
ante umbrales superiores.

VI.

Aurora,
tus ojos son el aire.
Se absorben
y sienten
en lo recóndito de un eco.
Aquél.

Vienes al mundo
abrevando largamente
en su respiración.
Has dragado esa laguna
de sonrisas, sorpresas,
temor, llanto, misterio:
te fluye entre los labios
el *nombre* de las cosas.

VII.

Así dispuestas,
las gotas suspendidas
en la punta de cada hoja
anuncian cielos,
sudarios del otoño o del invierno
que aún exhalan el deseo
de unirse al nuevo ser:

catarata de su risa,
cabello al aire de su lluvia torrencial,
lagrimeo constante de sus cuevas bajo tierra.

VIII.

Blanca.
casi nieve,
y tan húmeda
que no presagias nada,
desde tu cadáver fresco
te yergues sola,
resplandeciente,
resucitada inabarcable.

El bosque, la avenida, este jardín
han dejado el sepulcro atrás,
sus valles,
sus praderas empapadas
rumbo a la sequía del alma.
Un fulgor de llanto
brota de las ramas en cascada.
Cual ávidas serpientes,
los retoños se abren paso.
Se desliza su lenguaje.

IX.

Sobre tu paz,
ondula un velo adormecido,
vaporoso:

como un barco de amplias velas,
varado en la bahía interior,
mi cuerpo;
el tuyo,
marea siempre benigna
que humedece de transcurso
las entrañas.
Mi alegría es tal,
que casi llego a comprenderlo.

Qué escuchas,
me pregunto,
si no es canto
lo que sale de la boca,
sino hambre, sed sincera
de este muro
de lamentos
que es la piel.
Una sola de tus notas
quiso abrirme los oídos
y los ojos:
hablaría
llenándome de tiempo
en adelante.

X.

Mas el vacío penetra todo
y lo convierte en un emblema,
éter, mudanza humana.
Nada cambia el aparente
alivio de la fe.
Es deleznable
bienestar.
Polvo muy fino.

A punto de ver tu voz
en este sitio pleno
de alabanza natural
y serte inmune,
te vas, inapresable,
caballo que recorres
la sombra de unas huellas,
oculto en el tormento
de mis cascos.

Al transfigurarse

Después de aquella bruma,
el manantial puro del aire
se abre en flor ventricular,
iluminándose de lleno
el pasadizo.

Bienvenida.

Vas a derramar
espera eterna,
esperanza,

que ocurra,
que nazca,
que renazca.

Acaso muestres una ruta anticipada.
Acaso emprendas el sendero del calor,
desprovista ya
de aquel cuerpo doliente.
Acaso aprendas a gozar.

Bendita seas.

Déjame soñar
tu materia indisoluble,
tocar la frente al alba,
volver en mí, *a mí,*
siempre despierta.

III.
Intemperie

LOS CACHORROS

1.

Nubarrones, runas echadas,
este verano sólido,
padre paciente, manantial
de lo que viene ocurriendo
para seguir pasando,
esqueleto del magnífico
lugar común.
Este lugar.
Siluetas que se arrastran
por el mármol,
el mar del mal,
la mía entre ellas.
Hierbas, tercas florecillas.
Calcio de la muerte,
huesos fugitivos,
resplandores.

Varios cachorros de tigre entrelazados, dándose zarpazos, mordis-
queándose, lamiéndose los rasguños y volviendo al ataque, al juego,
a la cercanía de no sé qué con no sé qué. La tigresa, en aquel árido
paisaje, bajo un arbusto. Su majestad. De pronto, las cosas comen-
zaron a encarnizarse, a hacerse herida. El pelaje de la madre tem-
blaba aquí y allá. Alguna mosca, alguna abeja, algún insecto pertur-
bador. El cuerpo era una cosa y otra muy distinta su atención.
Quietud, percepción, libertad inalterada, curso prometido, desen-
volverse inevitable.

2.

Flor morada, de pétalos delgados,
cuatro pistilos al centro,
redondel amarillo madre.
Núcleo de los anales,

núcleo de la esperanza,
peso justo.

Cuatro criaturas, prendidas de una falda de vuelos amarillos. Cuatro
con destino, con mapa diseñado, maneras distintas de belleza, deu-
das. Por un instante, vuelven la vista al azul cielo, a la blancura que
lo enmarca, la gloria, y caen después al río rojo oscuro, casi negro.
"Había perdido tanta sangre en el momento de la autopsia que su
corazón estaba seco." Como un chabacano de los que se comen en
invierno, cuando se celebra la buena nueva. *Gloria in excelsis Deo.*

3.

Voces rotundas y masculinas
elevan melodías a la ausencia.
La cúpula y los muros
hacen del eco único sonido,
secuencia irrepetible,
goteo sobre la cabeza
del recién nacido.

Himnos de la víscera sellada
dentro de la burbuja del mundo.
Todo es vientre.
Todo, pila bautismal.
Ante ellos ella vuelve,
vuelve ya,
a su lugar de origen
sine qua non.
"Jóvenes, hagan el favor
de prestar algunas manos."
Es preciso tocar con las palmas
los filos de la Alianza.
Caja de pino,
perfecta para el rápido ocurrir
de lo que *tiene que ocurrir*
hoy,

porque el clima se refleja
en las inmensas lagunas de los actos.

Y ¿qué es de tu vida, persona en duelo? "El que come mi carne y
bebe mi sangre vive en mí y yo en él." Difícil de digerir. Una cruda,
otra sin destilar. Logré contener el asco porque vi a un hombre que
no había llorado aún. Desde el fondo del pozo de la tierra surgen a
borbotones los ojos chisporroteantes de los tigres niños. Se afilan
los colmillos. Devoran un muslo fresco de algún otro animal. "El
que come mi carne y bebe mi sangre no morirá para siempre."

4.

Los cadáveres azules en la nieve de Chechenia.
Los cadáveres cetrinos de la Selva Lacandona.
Los cadáveres color tierna cesárea.
La mirada cintilante de Osip, Josip, José,
clavada en la nuca de cada uno,
aunque en realidad buscara alimentarse,
un papel con algo escrito.
Las cenizas bibliotecales y el humo,
aún negro, de todos los libros,
todas las biografías de la tierra,
son faros entre los cuerpos
sin vida.
Sobre todo en los campos
de batalla.

LA MUERTE DEL BESO

Tú, oración,
tú, blasfemia,
tú, navaja en la oración
de mi silencio.

—PAUL CELAN

Fons

Quise hallarte dentro de mí
sabiendo que aquella oscura habitación
me deparaba vértigo en concavidades.
Quise, busqué tu rostro.
Quise de tal modo contemplar
la parte tuya dentro mío
que lograra atraer a las demás
y unir mi boca a otra, otras,
para ver cómo es el sueño.
Saber que en todo hay dos
salivas, ríos de vida,
fluyendo, influyéndose,
saber
qué sé, a qué sé,
lenguas de fuego sumergidas
en este mar de los misterios,
bañadas de oro
porque oro,
el Verbo se desprende hablado
y es muerte corporal escrita,
divina materia que besa eternamente
las espumas de una luz marina.
Mors osculi
hecha de amar, desear, sacar la cifra
pura, impura, lengua que dijo
En el principio,
conjugada y sublimada:
Soy el que soy,
ven a mí,

acércate con la boca abierta,
siente mi aliento,
llénate del Nombre,
abre los ojos y verás
Nada.

Origo

Espero afuera del salón de clases de tercero de primaria. El examen será oral, individual: triunfal. Todo el mundo tiembla. Se trata de una prueba de *lengua nacional*. Siento la boca seca, pastosa, el paladar partido. Soy toda gusto estéril, verdadera cornucopia ahogada. Entro. Cierro la puerta. Subo despacio a la tarima. "Conjuga lo que quieras en cualquier tiempo." Sin dudar un instante, *yacer* es la elección, presente imperfecto de mis con jugos. Transparente, revelada *exultó* mi lengua.

Fons

Reanimada, vuelta ánimo,
reincorporada, vuelta cuerpo,
contemplo entre sueños
una escena que he robado
como quien tomó el fuego,
como quien abrió la caja
de los males por curiosa,
como quien vio en sí misma
una igual al compañero,
el amor de su vida,
y se dispuso a hacerlo
sin esfuerzo de más.
Así tomé exactamente
lo que no era mío,
con los ojos.
Vi el mar en tus entrañas;
en tu superficie, el barro.
Te besé como un náufrago,
como quien insufla la palabra.
Recorrí con los labios
todo ese continente,
Adán, de tierra, Nada.
Me conocí en tu materia
aterrada,
desprendiendo aromático vapor,
amatorio banquete de cenizas.

Origo

Agencia de inhumaciones. Pregunto con insistencia a varias personas por separado: ¿qué quiere decir? Alguien me responde: enterrar. Otros me aconsejan guardar silencio. El vocablo exequias. La *voz* de las honras fúnebres. Me quedé pensando en humo y luego en humus y solté la carcajada. El día anterior había aparecido en un libro de ciencias naturales: materia orgánica completamente descompuesta, que forma parte de la tierra vegetal. Limo. Inhumar, sepultar, ¿tan pronto? Mejor querría acercarme a su mejilla. Oler su olor. Aunque así exhumara anhelos de corrupción.

Fons

Tendré que comer el pan,
beber el vino,
y viviré, ¿verdad?
Verdad.
De palabra y obra.
De obra en la palabra.
Doy mi palabra
y regresa a mi boca.
La trago, la digiero o la vomito.
Cuántas veces he dicho
mi ánimo está acercándose a la cima
del desconsuelo, no sé si pueda
bautizar al sufrimiento
y cuántas otras he vomitado
cómo lo siento
mi más sentido pésame.
Recuerdo, en cambio,
el agua viva, aquel deslumbramiento,
una de tantas noches
con el corazón latiendo tanto
que se veían sobre mi pecho
se angélico ascenso y su descenso,
es el corazón un espíritu puro
hecho de palabras digeridas.
Habla desde las fuerzas invisibles
e inasibles que suben y bajan
del manantial hasta el terror.
Un batir de alas más intenso
que el golpe certero del cincel.
Llega a la garganta, es eco
del poder sutil
      a heart murmur
del poder creador
      un soplo en el corazón
del poder que al sueño invita

the chambers of the heart
y del que expulsa de la vida
            los ventrículos del corazón.

Basta ya. La bomba repiquetea:
Salte de la diástole y la sístole.
Fuera, fuera de aquí.
La lengua del placer,
la del circunloquio espera,
no la del beso seminal
en las fauces del profeta:
"Y sucederá en los últimos días,"
dice Dios,
"que derramaré mi espíritu sobre toda carne,
y profetizarán vuestros hijos y vuestras hijas,
y vuestros jóvenes verán visiones,
y vuestros ancianos soñarán sueños."
En cada uno, un fragmento del cristal
significado.
Torre caída sobre hombre caído
sobre los granos de arena
que darán forma nuevamente
al muro de las lamentaciones,
a la muralla que cual *navaja en la oración* . . .
Una palabra Tuya bastará para sanar mi alma.
¿Cuál? ¿El soplo o el murmullo?
¿El aliento que da espíritu
o el sonido suave que predica
como viento entre las hojas?
Latidos, golpes sobre las puertas del cuerpo,
ábreme,
sobre los portones del mundo,
ciérrame,
sobre los umbrales todos.

Origo

Una es la pluma interior que explica cómo me voy consumiendo, conservando, transformando. Es. Otra, la que busca y encuentra respuestas allá afuera. Está. Pero, ¿en cuál articular la confesión? ¿Cómo desahogar un regodeo en algo que no sea *gaudium*? Ya me lo han hecho notar, esto es entregarse con avidez a un placer grosero. Un regodeo en des-entrañar. La boca del vicario tras las cortinitas emite un aire enrarecido que sugiere algo intraducible: *Preserve me, Oh Lord, in Thy mercy. For to know Thy Truth is Life.* Lenguas adentro y afuera, serpientes que se persiguen, se tocan, se besan, se desmoronan. Sus papilas son pupilas fijas en la búsqueda de un rostro. En ellas vive aquella agudísima nota, el éxtasis tan intenso que "a veces resulta, accidentalmente, en la muerte del cuerpo, un modo de morir conocido como la muerte del beso . . ."

Fons

Escritura al desnudo,
proyector de cuerpos opalinos.
Noches de lectura,
cultivo, culto de la Letra.
Oro en lenguas, murmuré,
para interpretar mi destino,
esa oscura asignación
de piel brillante y turbias carnes.
Fruto que se pudre al tocarlo,
al no quitar el dedo de renglón,
al no quitar el dedo de la llaga.
Estiro el brazo que habla
de ramificarse, bifurcarse,
de inscripciones en la lápida
del otro.
Brazo, parte cortada, amputada,
del beso.
Tabla de salvación,
soga al cuello,
tira de sábanas desde la ventana,
escapatoria entretejida con las venas
que de tanto estirarse se revienta.
Las voces de mi vida se han atado
una a la otra
como brazos cercenados:
intentar—estirar—alcanzar.
Las partes largas, lisas,
sí vencen las distancias.
Sus sílabas ahora me maldicen:

"Ya te alcanzaste,
te has estirado hacia ti misma,
cuán minúscula;
bienvenida al paraíso

de las perfectas omisiones,
al matiz disuelto en . . ."

¿A quién besas,
a quién tocas,
a quién te unes
don de fuego,
etéreo nudo corredizo?
Tras los velos de silencio
del lecho de la cámara profunda
se escucha la palabra del Amado:
soplo . . . breath . . .

Origo

Vientos apacibles hincharon las velas del barco que trajo a mi madre, después de un viaje no muy largo, hasta estas tierras de miseria adánica. Ahí, con ese imperceptible movimiento bajo los pies, fue aprendiendo a decir lo verdaderamente esencial: buenos días, buenas noches, hasta pronto . . . Traía por único equipaje el pequeño "cofre" que contenía su más preciado bien: una muñeca bellísima, réplica exacta de una niña como ella lo era entonces, con algunos vestiditos para las distintas ocasiones de la vida: del diario, de domingo . . . Llevaba su transcurso entre los brazos. Ignoro si habrá besado la tierra que la acogió, si su lengua madre se habrá llenado de excrecencias. Sólo Dios sabe cómo se habrá integrado a lo que la rodeaba en ese "Nuevo Mundo." Hace poco, alguien que mucho la besó en vida traficó con lo que en papel se define y describe como sus "restos áridos." Helo ahí: siempre abrigué el secreto conocimiento de que exhumar e inhumar habrían de ser la misma cosa. Cosa que con el vientecillo de una carcajada, humana como el humus, se *dis*grega, se *dis*persa, se *dis*loca, se hace aquí y ahora mi propio desquicio, *dis*late, voz sacada del antiguo deslatar, "disparar un arma," ambivalencia confirmada en testimonios del Siglo de Oro: *dis*late o *des*late: "shooting off," o bien, "a jest, a foolish speech."

Dramatis personae

Mi voz se fue amoldando a sus tejidos.
Se detuvo. Creyó no poder más
y continuó.
Conoció así un cauce
nunca antes descrito,
un lugar del que era parte
sin saberlo.
Al que volvió después.
Abrió sus puertas,
dio principio a los oídos.
Caracol de oleajes vigorosos,
saciaba todas las esperas
penetrando el cuerpo
en rojo intenso.

Luego tu voz ventisca,
desde las copas
de bosques invernales,
de huertos de la tundra,
desde el encino, el cedro
y desde el tamarindo,
atravesaba a los despiertos
que caminan
saboreando
la melodiosa sequedad
del trueno.

Dolor de corazón

¿Por qué erráis solitarios
por las embarcaciones y el campamento
en medio de la noche inmortal?

—Iliada, X, 139

La laguna de los muertos no tiene fin.
También la llaman río, gran Estigio.
Fluye cautelosa, cauteloso,
encandilando a sabios y creyentes.
Es lecho de ilusiones, de rumores,
se aloja fácilmente en los resquicios:
suelto espejismo
de humanos laberintos.

Intuyo su principio en esta barca, murmuré.
Sus tablones han dejado huellas en mis manos.
Los remos de la noche van hilando
la crisálida verdad del horizonte.

¿Es éste el ojo de agua
donde la diosa hundiera al hijo
para hacerlo invulnerable,
brutal, indiferente?
¿Es éste el Verbo
de seco lagrimal
que arrojó escudos por la borda?

IV.
Un cristal en otro

. . .

Una suerte de música inaudita
se abre paso, y desde dentro
nos despoja
de toda vestidura imaginable.
¿Soy ciego
o por primera vez observo
aquellos árboles de maravilla?
El fruto afina los colores,
resplandece.

Desde afuera mira el habitante

La piedra no es lo mismo para mí,
regresa sin forma a mi regazo
como mirada de soslayo,
alabanza en boca propia,
palabra madre.

No pesa más una piedra que una concha,
la contemplación nocturna
es capaz de convencernos;
la quietud no se comprende,
se escapa entre los dedos
y en falta de movimiento se transforma;
la oscuridad, terciopelo atemporal,
nos alivia, nos ayuda a prescindir
de explicaciones.
¿Por qué llorar, entonces?

¿De quién son las piedras del río
que ven tus ojos, habitante?
Tiene un espejo la mañana.
Helo aquí.

Has sembrado gozo, estaciones,
un árbol rojo, otro amarillo
y algunas ramas verdes todavía.
Otro sol vive al contacto con el cuerpo.
Al desenvolverse su fragancia
clava un alfiler en los sentidos;
una perla en el viento se desliza
y es de nuevo piedra,
sin sollozos,
habitante.

Te sigo

Verse sin el mundo,
no reconocerse en el espejo.
Qué frágiles,
qué endebles,
qué de carne y hueso somos.
Los mejores sentimientos se descubren
al recordar tangible a otro ser
cuya apariencia es ya intangible.
Cuán pequeñitos
nos tragamos el vacío,
lo tuyo sin ti,
yo.
Queremos llenarnos de una voz,
y escuchar ecos por dentro
que no cesan de soñar
en el retorno.
Feliz quien da la cara
a lo que se va
y se queda.

Pura López-Colomé (1952) nació en México, D.F. Estudió la licenciatura y la maestría en Letras Hispánicas e Hispanoamericanas en la UNAM. Poeta, traductora y ensayista, ha colaborado en revistas y suplementos nacionales y extranjeros. Ha publicado los siguientes poemarios: *El sueño del cazador* (Cuarto menguante Editores, 1985); *Un cristal en otro* (Ediciones Toledo, 1989); *Aurora* (Ediciones del Equilibrista, 1994); *Intemperie* (Ediciones Sin Nombre, 1997); *Éter es* (CONACULTA, Col. Práctica Mortal, 1999). Entre los autores a quienes ha traducido se encuentran William Carlos Williams, T. S. Eliot, Georg Trakl, Bertolt Brecht, Paul Celan, W. S. Merwin, Hilda Doolittle (H. D.), Robert Hass, Louise Glück, W. B. Yeats, Seamus Heaney. Vive en Cuernavaca.

Pura López-Colomé was born in Mexico City in 1952. She established herself as one of her generations' more important poets with her first book, *El sueño del cazador* (1985). Since then, she has gone on to publish several significant books—*Un cristal en otro* (1989), *Aurora* (1994), and *Intemperie* (1997)—distinguished by their concentrated syntax, their linguistic complexity, and their insistent moral and spiritual engagement. A literary critic and translator as well as a poet, she has rendered into Spanish major works by H. D., Virginia Woolf, Gertrude Stein, Samuel Beckett, and Robert Hass, among others. She lives with her husband, a scientist and musician, and their children, in Cuernavaca, Mexico.

Forrest Gander is the author of *Torn Awake* (New Directions, 2001); *Science & Steepleflower* (1998); *Deeds of Utmost Kindness* (1994); *Lynchburg* (1993); and *Rush to the Lake* (1988). He is the editor of *Mouth to Mouth: Poems by 12 Contemporary Mexican Women*, a bilingual anthology, and co-translator of *Immanent Visitor: Selected Poems of Jaime Saenz*. His criticism appears in the *Nation*, the *Boston Review*, and elsewhere. With poet and wife, C. D. Wright, he edits Lost Roads Publishers and currently directs the Graduate Creative Writing Program at Brown University. Among his honors and awards are a Whiting Award, two Gerturde Stein Awards for Innovative American Writing, and fellowships from the National Endowment for the Arts and Yaddo.

This book was designed by Wendy Holdman. It is set in Veljović, a typeface designed by Jovica Veljović and issued in 1984 by ITC. Composed by Stanton Publication Services, Inc., and manufactured by Hignell Book Printing on acid-free paper.

Graywolf Press is a not-for-profit, independent press. The books we publish include poetry, literary fiction, essays, and cultural criticism. We are less interested in best-sellers than in talented writers who display a freshness of voice coupled with a distinct vision. We believe these are the very qualities essential to shape a vital and diverse culture.

Thankfully, many of our readers feel the same way. They have shown this through their desire to buy books by Graywolf writers; they have told us this themselves through their e-mail notes and at author events; and they have reinforced their commitment by contributing financial support, in small amounts and in large amounts, and joining the "Friends of Graywolf."

If you enjoyed this book and wish to learn more about Graywolf Press, we invite you to ask your bookseller or librarian about further Graywolf titles; or to contact us for a free catalog; or to visit our award-winning web site that features information about our forthcoming books.

We would also like to invite you to consider joining the hundreds of individuals who are already "Friends of Graywolf" by contributing to our membership program. Individual donations of any size are significant to us: they tell us that you believe that the kind of publishing we do *matters*. Our web site gives you many more details about the benefits you will enjoy as a "Friend of Graywolf"; but if you do not have online access, we urge you to contact us for a copy of our membership brochure.

www.graywolfpress.org

Graywolf Press
2402 University Avenue, Suite 203
Saint Paul, MN 55114
Phone: (651) 641-0077
Fax: (651) 641-0036
E-mail: wolves@graywolfpress.org

Other Graywolf titles you might enjoy:

Warrior for Gringostroika by Guillermo Gómez-Peña
By Herself: Women Reclaim Poetry, edited by Molly McQuade
Antebellum Dream Book by Elizabeth Alexander
The Time of the Doves by Mercè Rodoreda,
    trans. by David H. Rosenthal
The Half-Finished Heaven by Tomas Tranströmer,
    trans. by Robert Bly